Note to Parents

This book provides young children with exciting, creative drawing and painting activities—and with some helpful "how-to" hints, as well.

Directions are simple and easy to follow. Younger children may need help with some activities, especially those that require cutting. The Jiminy Cricket symbol appears with projects that may require adult help.

Most materials are easy to find. You can save many kinds of paper for drawing and coloring—newspaper, paper grocery bags, and "shirt cardboard" from packaged clothing. Heavy, tough papers are best for painting. Avoid plastic-coated papers that repel crayon and paint.

Most other materials can be bought at dime stores. Poster paint is usually found in stationery or art supply stores. To make chalk drawings permanent, you can buy a fixative spray at art supply stores or use hair spray as an inexpensive substitute. Do the spraying yourself, in a well-ventilated room.

For carefree coloring and painting, provide your child with an old shirt and a "messproof" corner, well protected with newspaper. Then relax! Remember, there is no "right" or "wrong" in a child's art. Enjoy what your child spontaneously expresses through painting and drawing.

ISBN 0-7166-2901-1
Library of Congress Catalog Card No. 83-51333

Spatter
and Dash

Paint and Color Fun

Published by
World Book Encyclopedia, Inc.
a Scott Fetzer company
Chicago

The Blue-Footed Pink-Furred Hungry Baby

Morty and Ferdie took their painting stuff out of their backpacks and set up their easels on Horton's Hill.

"We'll be all ready first thing tomorrow morning when the sun comes up," said Ferdie.

"It'll be fun to paint the sunrise," said Morty.

Then they climbed into their sleeping bags and watched the moon rise. Before it sailed halfway across the sky, they were sound asleep.

Horton's Hill was still and dark. The night got even darker after the moon set, just before sunrise.

"AAaa-oooooo." The sound was like a big yawn.

Morty's eyes popped open. "It's okay to yawn," he said, "but do you have to wake a guy up?"

Ferdie's eyes were open, too. "I didn't yawn," he said. "Hey! If I didn't . . . and you didn't . . . who did?"

Morty shivered. Ferdie shivered. But they got up and looked around.

"Nothing here," said Morty. "We must've dreamed we heard someone yawn."

4

They wriggled back into their sleeping bags. But their eyes wouldn't close. "The sky is getting lighter," said Morty. "Sort of pinky purple."

"I see some red," said Ferdie.

"Un-gieeeee!" said a soft voice.

"I heard that," said Morty.

"So did I," said Ferdie.

Staying close together, they went looking. But they didn't find anyone.

Rays of pink and lavender and peach filled the sky. The clouds were fringed with gold.

"Wow!" said Ferdie. "Look at those colors! I'm going to paint the best sunrise anyone ever—"

"Ma-ma!" The soft sound floated in the quiet air.

Morty and Ferdie whirled around. Sitting in the shadow of a big rock was a small creature. It had blue feet and pink fur and an orange crest on its head.

"Ma-ma," it said and stuck its thumb in its mouth.

"What is it?" whispered Morty.

"I don't know," Ferdie whispered back. "But whatever it is, it's just a baby."

The baby got up and trotted toward them. "Un-gieee," it said. "Un-gieee."

"I think it's hungry," said Morty.

They got jelly sandwiches out of their backpacks and offered them to the baby.

The baby pushed them away. "Un-gieee," it wailed.

"What'll we feed it?" asked Ferdie.

"Most woods creatures eat grass," said Morty. He pulled up a handful of green shoots and held them out.

The baby shook its head. Then it saw a violet among the grass. Its eyes lit up. It popped the violet into its mouth. "Yummy!" it said softly.

"Hey!" said Morty. "It likes violets."

Morty and Ferdie hunted for more violets.

The hungry baby ate every one they found—nineteen in all—and said "yummy" after each one.

"If it likes violets," said Ferdie, "do you suppose it likes other flowers, too?"

"Yeah, but should it eat flowers?" asked Morty. "I mean, *we* aren't supposed to eat flowers."

"We eat jelly sandwiches, and it won't," said Ferdie. "So maybe flowers are what it's supposed to eat."

They found some black-eyed Susans. The hungry baby ate thirty-seven, smacking its lips.

Then Morty and Ferdie found tiger lilies and bluebells and Indian paintbrushes and daisies. The hungry baby ate seventy-four tiger lilies, a hundred and fifty-eight bluebells, two hundred and sixteen Indian paintbrushes, and four hundred and thirty-two daisies. It said "yummy" eight hundred and eighty times!

Morty and Ferdie flopped down on the grass.

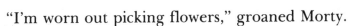

"I'm worn out picking flowers," groaned Morty.

"Besides, there aren't any left to pick," said Ferdie.

"Un-giee," wailed the baby. Tears spilled down its cheeks. It stuck its thumb in its mouth.

"What're we gonna do?" asked Ferdie.

"Maa-maa," the baby wailed softly.

Morty and Ferdie looked at each other. They bounced to their feet and cupped their hands around their mouths. "Maa-maa," they called as loudly as they could. "Maa-maaaa!"

They listened.

A sound came from far away. Thump . . . thump . . . .

"Maa-maa!" Morty and Ferdie called again.

The noise got louder. *Thump . . . thump . . . .*

"One more time," said Ferdie, his teeth chattering.

"Maa-maaaa!" they called. Then they dived into their sleeping bags and covered their heads.

Noises filled the air. THUMP . . . rustle . . .
THUMP . . . rustle . . . THUMP! The thumpings and
rustlings stopped nearby.

"Mama!" said a happy-sounding little voice.

"Ba-by!" said a happy-sounding big voice.

Morty and Ferdie each uncovered one eye and
peeked.

The hungry baby's mother was holding it in one arm.
In the other, she carried a huge rustly bunch of flowers.
She gave the baby an orange flower.

"Yummy," said the baby, munching away.

The baby's mother looked toward the sleeping bags.
Morty and Ferdie covered their eyes again.

THUMP . . . rustle . . . THUMP . . . rustle . . . .
The sounds stopped beside the sleeping bags. There
was a lot of rustling. Then the footsteps moved away,
getting softer and softer. THUMP . . . rustle . . . *thump*
. . . rustle . . . thump . . . .

The baby's voice grew softer, too. *Yum . . . yum . . . .*

It was a long time before Morty and Ferdie spoke.
"You want to look first?" Ferdie asked at last.

"Nope. You look first."

"Let's look together. One, two, three—"

They uncovered their eyes at the same time. The
hungry baby was gone. So was its mother. Morty and
Ferdie sat up. Beside each of their sleeping bags was a
bunch of flowers, beautiful flowers the like of which
they had never seen before.

"I think its mama tried to say thanks," said Ferdie.

The sun was high in the blue sky.

As they stuffed their paints into their backpacks,
Morty said, "We didn't see the sunrise."

"We saw something better," said Ferdie.

When We Were Little

"Tell us about the olden days," said Morty.

"About when we were little," said Ferdie.

So Mickey told them about when they were small. "Remember how you boys liked to fingerpaint?" he said. "It was a good way to start painting. You wore my old shirts buttoned down the back for smocks, but you got paint all over yourselves anyway.

"You always made big, round suns, Morty," he went on. "And you liked to paint flowers, Ferdie."

"Pluto fingerpainted, too," said Morty. "Remember, Uncle Mickey?"

"No, he didn't," said Ferdie. "He paw painted!"

Fingerpainting is easy and fun. Here are some things to try with finger paints.

Jiminy Cricket says, "For very young children, make finger paint with instant pudding mix. It's safe and delicious for thumb-in-mouth toddlers."

What you'll need

Liquid starch	Shelf paper
Food coloring	Sponge
Plastic cups	Water

1. Fill a cup half full with liquid starch. Add drops of food coloring to make finger paint. Fill another cup with water.

2. Lay the shelf paper shiny side up. Wet the paper all over with the sponge.

3. Spread some finger paint on the paper. Smooth it with your whole hand.

4. Now paint with your fingers. Use one finger to make lines. Bunch your fingers to make flowers or leaves on trees.

5. When your painting is finished, lay it on clean newspaper to dry.

"Remember that big bunch of balloons Uncle Mickey painted on your bedroom wall?" Minnie said. "That was how you learned your colors."

"I remember," Morty said. "My favorite one was orange."

"Remember how you learned to mix paints?" Minnie asked.

"I sure do," Morty answered. "We learned to make lots of colors by mixing red and blue and yellow. I learned to mix orange right away!"

"Remember how we made prints with your vegetables?" said Ferdie.

"I'll never forget that," Minnie told him. "I gave you chunks of carrots. You dipped them in poster paint and made prints on paper—car wheels and suns and flowers."

"And then we tried all kinds of things," Ferdie said. "Slices of onion, pieces of potato, celery, cabbage . . . ."

"And a big green bean for a smile," Morty added.

Jiminy Cricket says, "Ask a grown-up to cut the vegetables for you."

13

Good-Looking Pictures

Quiet! Artists at work! Morty and Ferdie are painting a great new picture—*Brave Watchdog on Duty*. Look closely and you'll see how they make their pictures.

Morty and Ferdie can see that most of the things they are drawing have one or two big shapes. So they start their drawing with shapes like these:

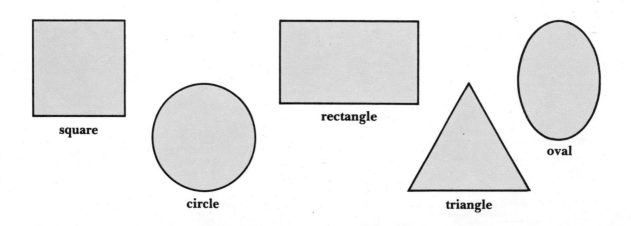

square

circle

rectangle

triangle

oval

Morty and Ferdie draw lightly with a pencil, so that they can erase if they need to. A treetop is usually a circle or a triangle. Some bushes are circles, too.

A house is usually a square or rectangle. A triangle on top makes a pointed roof.

The cat's head is a circle. So is its body—when it isn't running from Pluto.

Pluto is made up of lots of big and little ovals—and a long hot-dog shape.

When the big shapes are all in place, Morty and Ferdie add the smaller parts of the picture. They smooth out some lines, and they erase the lines they don't need. Then they are ready to color.

Let's watch the artists at work on a
picture of a famous mouse of long
ago—their Great-Great-Great Uncle
Christopher. (Mickey is posing for the
picture, of course.)

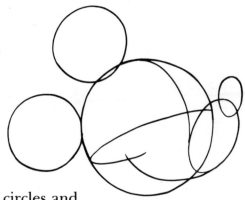

Mickey's head is mostly circles and
ovals. Morty and Ferdie start like this.

Morty and Ferdie start drawing
Mickey's body, hands, and feet with
ovals, too.

Then they change the shapes a little
and add a few lines.

Finally Morty and Ferdie add some
exciting touches—a sword, a medal,
and a very fancy, old-fashioned hat.
(After all, Great-Great-Great Uncle
Christopher was a famous explorer!)

Mickey is really impressed with the finished picture!
"Handsome, isn't he?" Mickey says whenever he looks at
it.

   "You look just like him," Morty and Ferdie answer.

   Try making your drawings the same way Morty and
Ferdie do. First draw the big shapes with pencil. Then
add or change the lines until your drawing looks the
way you want it to look. Now add the finishing touches
and color your picture. Soon you'll be making good-
looking pictures of your own.

Crayon Fun

Morty's crayons were brand new. Ferdie's were old.

Morty's crayons all had sharp points, but Ferdie's crayons were broken into many different lengths. Most of them had blunt, flat ends.

Who would draw the best picture?

Morty drew a lion. He made a big, beautiful outline. But how could he fill it in? The sharp points on his crayons weren't good for that.

Ferdie drew a beautiful green field. He used the side of his green crayons to make the grass smooth. He left open places to add flowers and a tree and a bee. But he couldn't draw the flowers and the tree and the bee. His stubby crayons weren't good for that.

"Want to trade?" asked Morty. "You can use my pointy crayons to make your flowers and the bee."

"You can use my flat orange crayons to fill in your lion," said Ferdie.

So Morty and Ferdie traded crayons. With Morty's long, pointed crayons and Ferdie's bits and pieces, they made two perfect pictures.

Here are some of the things Morty and Ferdie did with their crayons. You can do them, too.

You can make a smooth, even background with the side of a crayon.

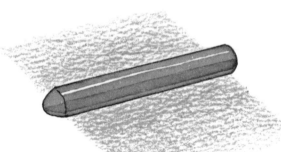

Use the pointed ends of crayons for eyes and noses and mouths and the center of flowers.

Draw a flower using just the side of a crayon. Make one edge of each petal darker by pressing hard on one side of your crayon.

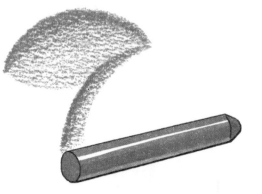

Fill in rounded shapes with curving strokes. Fill in long or tall shapes with long, straight strokes.

All Wet

"My octopus looks like it's on land," said Morty.

"Mine looks like it's on a blue blanket," said Ferdie. "Shucks, Uncle Mickey. What are we doing wrong?"

"You're really not doing anything wrong," Mickey told them. "But there's a special way to make watery pictures look wet and misty. When we go home, I'll show you."

Morty and Ferdie could hardly wait to get started. At home, they watched Mickey draw a picture like theirs. Then Mickey got a pan of water and a big sponge.

"Hey—you're getting your picture all wet!" Ferdie said.

"That's right," Mickey answered. "Now, watch what happens when I paint."

OCTOPUS

"It works!" Ferdie whispered to Morty.

"Gee, thanks, Uncle Mickey," Morty said. "Two wet-looking octopuses, coming up!" And he and Ferdie ran to get their paints.

Morty and Ferdie thought of lots of misty pictures to paint—haunted houses, ghosts, a cat in a fog, and all kinds of things in a snowstorm. Try making pictures like theirs—or try some ideas of your own.

First draw your picture lightly in pencil. Tape your picture to a drawing board. Wet the picture with clear water.

Paint your lightest color first. Move the picture to help the color spread.

Let the picture dry a little. Then fill in deeper colors on the octopus. The colors will blur at the edges.

Let the picture dry a little and add the darkest colors to faces or shadows.

Helpful Hints
from Uncle Mickey

"Wow, Uncle Mickey," Morty said. "Look at that picture! I can't paint like that. Real artists must know a lot of secret tricks."

Mickey laughed. "There really aren't any secret tricks, Morty," he said. "But there are some helpful hints I can give you. And I'll tell you a secret. A lot of real artists started painting the same way you did."

"Really, Uncle Mickey?" Morty said.

"Really and truly," Mickey told him. "And when some of those artists were kids, I'll bet they didn't paint as well as you do now. So keep on trying. Maybe you will paint like that someday."

Here are some of the helpful hints Mickey gave Morty. You can use Mickey's tips to make your good pictures even better.

Let the paper show through the color—on purpose! Your painting will seem to sparkle.

Painting a leaf isn't as hard as it looks. You press down on the brush, move it along gently, and lift it for the tip of the leaf.

Which part of the apple is shiniest? Wipe away some paint with a tissue to make that spot lighter. This gives the apple an interesting "shine."

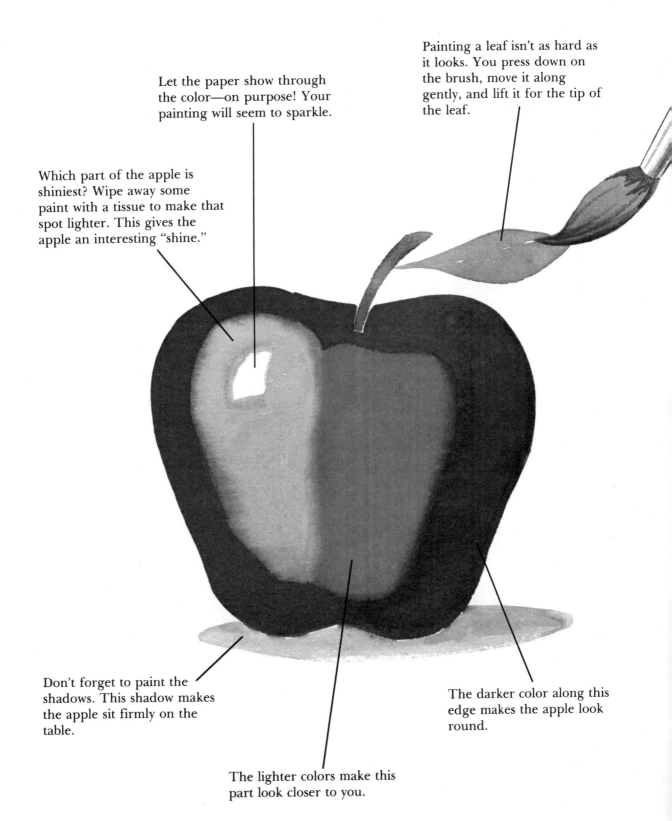

Don't forget to paint the shadows. This shadow makes the apple sit firmly on the table.

The darker color along this edge makes the apple look round.

The lighter colors make this part look closer to you.

 Jiminy Cricket says, "Make
sure it's okay to paint on the
mirror. And ask a grown-up to
help you cut out eye places on
the cowboy face."

In a Mirror

Every time Morty and Ferdie looked in a mirror, they saw two faces exactly alike. "No wonder people can't tell us apart," Morty said. "When I look in the mirror, I can't tell us apart, either."

One day they decided to change that. Ferdie used poster paints to paint a clown face on the mirror. He left openings for the eyes so that he could look in the mirror and see himself as a clown.

Morty cut a cowboy face out of paper. He colored the mouth and nose and cut openings for the eyes. He taped the face to the mirror. Then he cut out a cowboy hat and scarf and taped those to the mirror, too.

After that when Morty and Ferdie looked in their mirror, they didn't see two exactly alike faces. They saw Funny Bone Ferdie and Morty of the Lone Trail.

Use poster paint to make your clown face. Leave quite big openings for the eyes.

Use different colored papers for the cowboy face and hat and scarf. You can color in or paste on a mouth and nose and eyebrows—and a big mustache if you want one!

Using Your Imagination

"Hey," Ferdie said to Minnie. "You're painting flowers—but I don't see any flowers around here."

"Yeah," said Morty. "I thought you needed to see something to paint it."

Minnie laughed. "I'm wishing I had a great big bouquet of flowers, so I'm painting one," she said. "It's fun to paint things you see in your mind. That's called using your imagination. Sometimes the pictures that come from your imagination are the best pictures of all."

So Morty and Ferdie used their imaginations. They painted pictures of things as they'd like them to be.

Can you use your imagination to make a picture? Be sure to sign your name to your picture. After all, *you* imagined it!

Morty painted his own picture—as Mortimer the Magnificent.

Ferdie painted a picture of the dragon
he will capture—if he ever finds one.

Listen to a Rainbow

What is Pink?

What is pink? A rose is pink
By the fountain's brink.
What is red? A poppy's red
In its barley bed.
What is blue? The sky is blue
Where the clouds float through.
What is white? A swan is white
Sailing in the light.
What is yellow? Pears are yellow,
Rich and ripe and mellow.
What is green? The grass is green,
With small flowers between.
What is violet? Clouds are violet
In the summer twilight.
What is orange? Why, an orange,
Just an orange!

Christina Rossetti

Red stockings, blue stockings,
Shoes tied up with silver;
A red rosette upon my breast
And a gold ring on my finger.

Old Nursery Rhyme

Daffy-down-dilly is now come to town
With a petticoat green and a bright yellow gown.

Old Nursery Rhyme

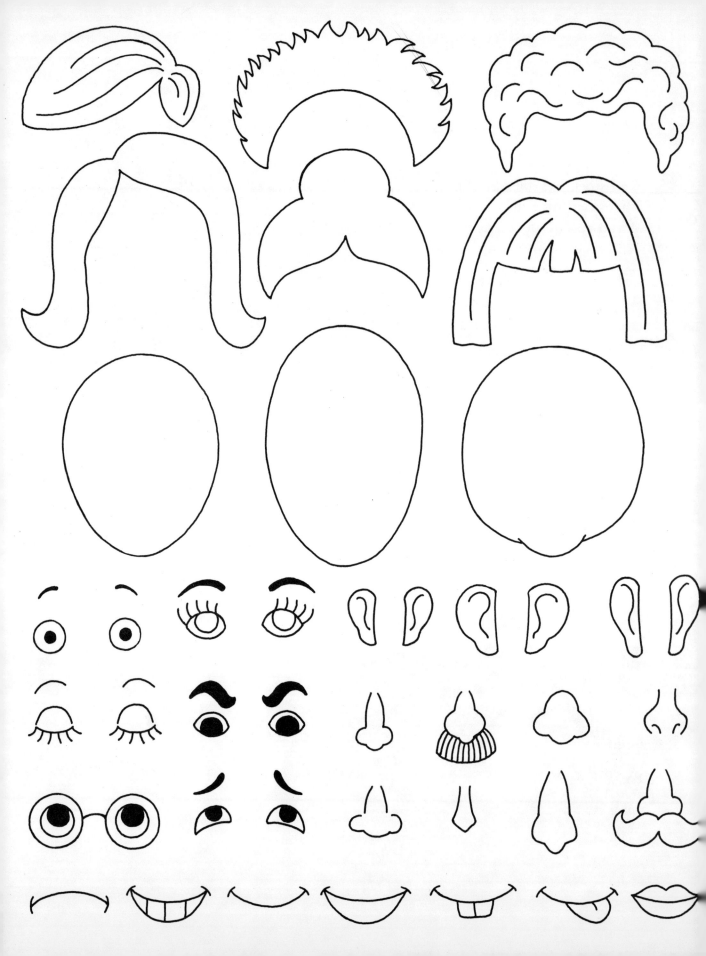

What's in a Face?

Mickey thinks it's fun to draw all kinds of faces—happy ones, sad ones, and even mad ones. The happier, sadder, or madder he makes them, the funnier they get.

To show you how he gets started, Mickey drew several face shapes here. Then he drew different kinds of eyes, mouths, and noses to fit into the faces.

Pick one of the face shapes. Trace it on any paper that's thin enough to see through. Then trace eyes, a mouth, a nose, and hair. Add a hat or scarf if you want one.

You can make a laughing face, or a sad face, or a surprised face. You can mix up the expressions, too. You can make a face with a laughing mouth and surprised eyes, or a face with laughing eyes and a sad mouth.

You can draw hundreds of different faces with these shapes. And you can make up shapes of your own.

Jiminy Cricket says, "Don't draw in your book! Always trace the faces on paper."

31

Rub It In!

What a beautiful day! It's too nice to stay inside, so
Morty and Ferdie are taking their crayons for a walk.
They're going to make a kind of picture called a *rubbing*.

Rubbings are easy to make. Morty and Ferdie look for
things that have a raised, bumpy-feeling pattern—
bricks, wood, rocks, weeds, or leaves like these.

They lay the leaves on a piece of heavy cardboard
. . . place a sheet of paper on top . . . and rub the
side of a crayon over the paper.

Here is a spring picture. Morty made the leaf rubbings with bright green crayons. To add the "cloud," he made a rubbing on a rough sidewalk.

Look for more things to try. Then make some rubbings of your own.

Look-Alikes
Don't See Alike

Morty and Ferdie stood in front of a mirror.

"You've got my eyes," said Morty.

"You've got my nose," said Ferdie.

"We look exactly alike," said Morty. "I wish we were different."

Mickey heard them. "Each of you draw a picture of Pluto," he said. "Don't show each other your pictures. Just bring them to me. Now scoot."

Ferdie colored his picture carefully. "My picture looks exactly like good ole Pluto," he said.

Morty painted away. "So does mine. Nice old Pluto," he said, "the friendliest dog anywhere."

Pluto opened one eye. He smiled and twitched his ears. He thumped his tail on the ground.

When they were finished, Morty and Ferdie took their pictures to Mickey. He set them side by side and

he laughed and laughed. "You look alike," he said, "but
you sure don't see alike!"

   You and a friend can do what Morty and Ferdie did.
Draw pictures of the same thing. (No fair peeking!)
When you are finished, look at the drawings side by
side. What different things did each of you see?

Spatter and Spray

Morty and Ferdie watched Minnie make a colorful picture—without ever touching her paintbrush to the paper. "That's a funny way to paint," said Morty.

"It's a *fun* way to paint," Minnie told him. "This is a spatter painting. Get your watercolors, and I'll show you how to make one."

Morty and Ferdie drew some designs on cardboard and cut them out. (Ferdie made a simple design. Morty used his initials—MM.) Then Minnie showed them what to do.

When they were finished, Morty had a sign for the door of his room. Ferdie had a picture for Pluto. And they both had lots of ideas for other designs to spatter and spray.

What you'll need

Watercolor   Cardboard
Paintbrush   Tape
Jar of water   Paper

1. On the cardboard, draw a design that has big, simple shapes.

2. Cut out the shapes and arrange them on your paper. Make sure the pieces lie flat.

3. Dip your brush in paint. Shake off the big drops. Then hold your brush over the paper and tap it gently against your other hand. Drops of paint will spatter onto the paper.

4. Keep moving and tapping the brush until the paper is covered with dots.

5. Let the color dry. If you like, you can add more spatters of another color.

6. When all the colors are dry, lift the shapes off the paper. Your picture is ready to hang.

 Jiminy Cricket says, "Be sure you spread out lots of newspaper when you spatter-paint."

Color Up a Storm

One day Morty drew a picture of his favorite old teddy bear. He'd had that bear ever since he was a baby.

"That's a great picture," said Ferdie.

"Well, it's okay," Morty replied. "But I wish I could make it look fuzzy and soft, the way it really is. I'm going to ask Uncle Mickey how to do it."

Mickey had just what Morty needed—a big box of colored chalk. "Chalk is something like crayons, because

Morty drew his favorite old toy, his bear. He gave his bear a parachute. He rubbed the colors with his finger to mix them and make his teddy bear look soft.

you can color with it," Mickey explained. "But it's something like paints, too. You can blend the colors, and you can make things look soft and fuzzy—like your teddy bear."

Morty tried the colored chalk. He made a soft, fuzzy picture of his bear. Ferdie wanted to use lots of colors— so he colored up a soft, glowing rainbow. "Gee, Uncle Mickey—it works fine!" they said.

You can think of lots of good ways to use colored chalk. Maybe you'd like to draw a picture of a soft, fuzzy pet. Chalk is good for drawing faces, too.

Jiminy Cricket says, "Ask a grown-up to spray your best chalk drawings with fixative or hair spray. It keeps the chalk from rubbing off."

Ferdie used the sharp edge of the chalk for the leaves and apples on the tree. He used the side of the chalk to make the colors in his rainbow.

Tickle Me Pink

Morty: What's green with purple spots and has a glowing red nose and yellow eyes?

Ferdie: I don't know.

Morty: Neither do I, but there's one standing right behind you.

What do they call little orange cats in Greenland?

Kittens.

Mickey: What colors shall I paint the winds and the waves in this picture?

Minnie: The winds blue and the waves rose.

Why are elephants gray?

Because they look terrible in pink.

Why is that elephant wearing pink
ballet slippers?

Because she can't dance in pink tennis shoes.

What's black and white and red all
over?

An embarrassed panda.

Can you name four yellow animals?

Three lions and a scared duck.

The Great Glue-Up

Mickey looked puzzled. "I can't find my old baseball cap," he said. "This morning I couldn't find that old sketch of Pluto. And Pluto's Dog of the Year Award is missing, too."

"My old straw hat is gone," said Minnie. "So are those seashells we found at the beach. And the pictures Morty and Ferdie painted have disappeared. I think we have a mystery here!"

Pluto heard Mickey and Minnie. He put his nose to the floor and sniffed. He sniffed all the way to Morty and Ferdie's bedroom door. Then he sat up and barked.

Ferdie opened the door. The mystery was solved.

"We made a glue-up picture without any paints," said Morty. "We just used glue and a lot of things we like."

"The glue-up will help us remember happy times," said Ferdie.

You can make a picture to help you remember happy times, too.

What you'll need

Cardboard	Pictures and other favorite things	Yarn
Colored paper	Glue	

1. Cut a piece of colored paper the size of your cardboard. Glue it to the cardboard.

2. Arrange your happy things on the cardboard the way you want them. Glue them in place. Let the glue dry.

3. Punch two holes at the top of your picture. Thread yarn through the holes. Leave a big enough loop to hang the picture. Tie the yarn in a bow. Now your picture is ready to hang.